TALK MORE
SAY LESS
GET AHEAD

TALK MORE
SAY LESS
GET AHEAD

The business-speak dictionary

HarperCollins*Publishers*

HarperCollins*Publishers*
1 London Bridge Street
London SE1 9GF

www.harpercollins.co.uk

HarperCollins*Publishers*
1st Floor, Watermarque Building, Ringsend Road
Dublin 4, Ireland

First published by HarperCollins*Publishers* 2021

1 3 5 7 9 10 8 6 4 2

© HarperCollins*Publishers* 2021

Illustrations by Joelle Avelino

Harriet Dobson asserts the moral right to
be identified as the author of this work

A catalogue record of this book is
available from the British Library

ISBN 978-0-00-843413-7

Printed and bound in the UK using
100% Renewable Electricity at CPI Group (UK) Ltd

MIX
Paper from
responsible sources
FSC™ C007454

This book is produced from independently certified FSC™ paper
to ensure responsible forest management.

For more information visit: www.harpercollins.co.uk/green

For all those who hold the career
ladders of others as they climb higher
and higher to success ...

IT'S TIME TO LET GO

CONTENTS

Introduction
Adopting the Language of Leaders   1

Dictionary of Terms A–L   5

How to Out-riddle a Riddler and
Other Useful Tips   57

Dictionary of Terms M–Z   71

Bonus BS Bingo and Other Activities   119

ADOPTING THE LANGUAGE OF LEADERS

Whether you're new to the world of work or you just want to brush up on your leadership lingo, we're here to help. Conveniently sized to fit into the pockets of any power suit, this book will allow you to translate your colleagues' confusing, yet persuasive, choices of language without any of them realising what you're *really* fumbling with underneath that meeting table.

Soon, you too will have the confidence to repeat phrases like these, without a hint of embarrassment or irony:

Let's fry some ideas in the thought wok and see what sizzles.

*Let's look under the bonnet of this project
to really get these wagons circling.*

*Action that! (Even if you're not totally
clear on what 'that' is.)*

Helping you leap up that career ladder as if it were a strategic staircase to Inspiration Boulevard, this book will allow you to both ask and answer all of the questions you hadn't thought to ask, because you hadn't really understood them, including:

*How much bucketising is too much
bucketising?*

*When is it appropriate to 'put on a record
to see who dances' in a strictly business
scenario?*

*Is punching a puppy always the best
approach to winning a deal?*

But as we all know, the best questions are left unanswered, so this book will leave you to devise your own answer to the following question:

Why do we speak this way?

So, dive into these pages as if your career depends on it, because it does.

Action that!

This can be said in response to any idea – no matter your level of seniority. Make sure to yell it enthusiastically and accompany it with a heavy-handed point at whoever you think spoke last. It is particularly effective if you stand up and leave the room immediately afterwards.

Agile working

Meaning you can work from anywhere at all – a coffee shop, a sofa, a bed, the cupboard where you usually go to cry, the corner you crouch in when your weekly panic attacks hit, the beach, etc. In a cruel twist of irony, agile working actually makes you much, *much* less agile; your shoulders hunch, leg cramps become the norm and if you have any strength left in your arms at all, you'll start involuntarily waving goodbye to any feeling in your buttocks.

Al desko

A play on the Italian 'al fresco', the literal translation of which is 'in the cool'. Al desko is where one sits at one's desk slurping lunch all over the keyboard while watching one's inbox pile up at a staggering velocity. The first rule of eating al desko is to tell everybody you've eaten al desko – this will give you extra brownie points with the boss and make your colleagues feel guilty about their 10-minute dash to PRET.

All sizzle no steak

This can be used to describe anything that hasn't reached the high expectations you pinned to it six months ago. Realising your mistake, you might swivel at dangerous speed on your swivel chair, desperately searching for somebody to blame. Jason might catch your eye, and before you have time to remember whether or not this was his project, you might say:

No, Jason, it's not good enough – these numbers are all sizzle, no steak, which is what I predicted months ago!

Be sure to whip back around for maximum effect.

Analysis paralysis

Workers spend on average 66% of their working week in a state of analysis paralysis. It describes the act of overthinking every possible outcome of a situation to the point where nothing gets accomplished at all. In short, it's a creativity killer.

So when next you find yourself at the end of another of your mediocre presentations, instead of sweating your way through garbled answers to fill the time that somebody stupidly allotted for questions, just hold up both hands, arrange your face into a warm yet patronising smile and say:

*Look, guys, we're in danger of
analysis paralysis here. No further
questions, please.*

Keep those hands raised as you back up slowly through
the nearest exit.

AOB

Traditionally known as the time allotted to discuss Any
Other Business at the end of a meeting. True leaders will
ignore the pleading eyes and turbulent fidgets of their
colleagues and will instead choose this moment to raise
a complicated discussion point that will take at least
fifteen minutes to untangle and resolve.

If you require a volunteer for a project, this is the best
time to source one. Your weaker-bladdered co-workers
will be so desperate to leave the meeting, they'll agree to
do absolutely anything.

B

Backburner

Your work backburner is a document or folder where the worst of your very average ideas go to live in a state of purgatory. Not quite bad enough to be written off completely, not quite good enough to be spoken about publicly – other than to be muttered to your boss when you realise there are still seven minutes left of your weekly catch-up and you've run out of good–average things to say. Your backburner is also a great place to compile a list of tasks for whoever is to replace you when you retire. It's best to start this list on the very first day of your career and just keep adding to it, unrewarding decade after unrewarding decade.

Balls in a jam jar

If a competitor or client has your company's collective balls in a jam jar, it's likely an emergency meeting will be called to extract them. Essentially it means your hands are tied, but it's much worse because instead of your hands, it's your balls; and instead of a rope, it's a transparent jar that can be paraded around for all to see. Remember: nothing can be more reputationally damaging than indecent exposure. If during the emergency meeting you sense that your colleagues aren't taking this quite as seriously as they ought, be sure to up the level of hysteria by slamming your hand down on the table and yelling:

They've got our balls in a jam jar and the wasps are coming, people!

Bleeding edge

The newest, most groundbreaking thing ever. Think 'cutting edge' but bloodier and therefore instantly more thrilling/profitable. You could say:

This new range of children's toys is the
bleeding edge of educational development.

And nobody would be worrying about the damaging effect they could have on children's hands.

Boil an ocean

If you want to 'boil an ocean', then you want to do the seemingly impossible, like persuade your desk neighbour to type at a normal volume or get your manager to stop opening every conversation with, 'Can I ask you a quick question?'. Others will say it can't be done, but with 20/20 vision and the foresight to take the long view, you sense that boiling oceans will soon become just another tale on your newsfeed. You see the possibilities that others don't and can start looking forward to telling your colleagues you told them so, right before you burn together in that hot, hot lava.

Example sentence:

They said this new environmental policy
would be like boiling an ocean, but I just
don't think they wanted to handle the heat.

Feeling out of your depth? Then you're doing it right.

Brainstorm

See instead: *Ideate*.

Brand trajectory

A brand trajectory is the vague direction in which you want your company's visibility and profitability to go. Just like the number of zeros on your payslip and a hot air balloon (before its planned descent), brand trajectories are only supposed to go one way: up, up, up. So whenever you are asked the question, 'What does your brand trajectory look like?', feel free to throw your interlocuter a smirk and point enthusiastically to the sky until they walk away.

See also: *Narrative*.

Bucketisation

The bucketisation of something is the act of dividing it up into categories to make it more manageable. If, for example, you find yourself delegating tasks as part of a particular project and you get a whiff of Susan's ambition to take the lead on something you'd assigned to your own bucket, you can approach Susan and stage-whisper:

Get out of my bucket, Susan.

If she doesn't back up immediately, it's perfectly normal office practice to hit her with the nearest spade you can get your shaking hands on.

Calendarise

To calendarise is to add something to a digital calendar. In recent years it has come to replace the equally detested term 'diarise'. It's important to ask yourself: if a meeting wasn't in your calendar, did it really happen?

The answer is, of course, no. No, it did not. The following are all perfectly valid uses of the term:

> *Sure, let's calendarise something for next week.*

> *I'll contact her PA so we can calendarise tomorrow's lunch.*

> *I'm going to retroactively calendarise that meeting we just had so that neither of us can deny it happened.*

Catch it in the success net

Every worker has their own individual success net, but you must *always* refer to your success net as if it were a *collective* success net. It's normal for all employees to keep up the age-old pretence that success is something that can be *shared*. Next time you're in a big meeting and somebody has a brilliant idea, at the very end, just when everybody thinks it's all over, punch the air and loudly exclaim:

Let's catch this baby in our success net!

The louder you shout, the more likely it is that people will attribute the idea to you.

Circle back

The act of agreeing to talk about something again at a later point in the day/week/month/year/millennium. The trick to circling back is to keep going round and round the circle, over and over the same topic, until your co-workers get so dizzy they vomit.

Clear the deck

If your to-do list is filling up with things you simply don't want to do, you can just invent a new, very important, task to focus all your energy and efforts onto. It's best to give this task a nickname or acronym so people will assume they're supposed to know all about it and are less likely to ask questions. If, for example, Sam requests that report you promised her two months ago, just say:

Sorry, Sam, I had to clear the deck to focus on the B.S. job, so you'll have to ask Jordan to dive into the sea and fish out that report.

Clicks and mortar strategy

Your clicks and mortar strategy is the act of selling something online and face-to-face. Think of yourself as a door-to-door salesperson with a wi-fi connection. If you want to do a business deal, it's advisable to turn up at your correspondent's office, and while you're pitching to them in person, spam them over email with the exact same words until they relent or call security.

Close of play

This is the time when all that play you've been doing all day has to come to an end and you finally need to send a few emails.

See also: *Magic hour*.

Cloudwash

If you want to make something sound up to date, just add the prefix 'cloud-' to its name, e.g. *cloud-computing, cloud-orienteering, cloud-waxing, cloud-mopping*. Only a fool would question your meaning in public.

Come full circle

At some point in your three-hour-long meeting, it will become apparent that your team has talked around an issue so much that you are back where you started. The moment you realise what has happened, the race is very much on to be the first to point this out. First prize is exemption from blame, which means it is up to the others to find a swift resolution.

Just like when you're playing a tense game of *Snap* with your precocious niece, shriek *FULL CIRCLE* at the top of your lungs to show that the way to *really* win, is to win loudly.

D

Decompose to a lower level of granulation

This is another way of saying 'let's look at this a little more closely' but in a more opaque and therefore more leader-like way. Enjoy the three or so seconds your colleagues take to figure out what it is that you're asking them to do. These seconds of glory are what being a leader is all about. You might say:

Great idea, Karim, but can we decompose that to a lower level of granulation and roll around in the soil in a totally platonic way, please?

Deep dive

If you want to take a deep dive into something, you need to be willing to dedicate at least twenty minutes to the task, and that doesn't include the time you'll spend procrastinating when you're supposed to be donning that wetsuit and flippers.

You might, for example, be asked to take a deep dive into the actions of your competitors. This simply means you need to spend a quarter of an hour on their website and a further five minutes scrolling their social media feeds before writing up a report fluffing out the little evidence you've acquired with good old-fashioned guesswork. When feeding back to your team, remember to act like you've been to the back of beyond and seen things they couldn't even imagine.

Dialogue

To discuss, to converse, to chat, but in a painfully cool way.
   Example sentence:

> *Let's dialogue about this offline over a
> couple of mocha-latte-frappés.*

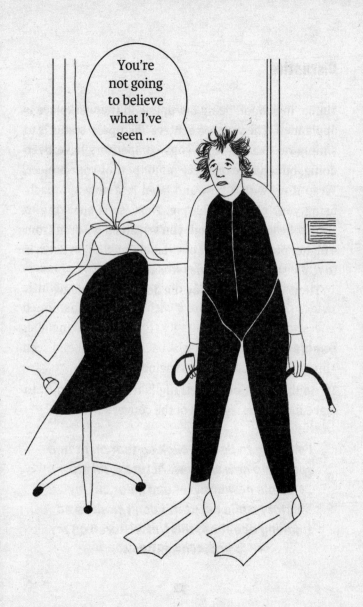

Disruptive

Unlike in school, being disruptive in the workplace is applauded. The way you achieve 'disruptor' status is to simply do exactly what your competitors have been doing, but change *one* very minor part of your project. Wrap it up with a bow and label it 'a new approach' using your cleanest Sharpie. Next, start speaking to your colleagues as though you've gained wisdom from a higher power and your one remaining task on Earth is to really shake up the sales strategy for Q3.

Then sit back and enjoy the deafening applause.

Double-click

To double-click on something is to home in on it, to make it the primary focus of the conversation, e.g.:

I'm going to double-click on that point and open up a new window. Actually, I'll start a whole new browser and clear out my history while I'm at it. I don't want to be thinking about anything else stored on my computer right now.

Drill down

If you want to drill down into something, you want to get beyond the bottom of an issue, all the way down to the heart of the matter, so that before you know it, you're at the core. It'll be so dark down there, you won't remember why or how you started drilling in the first place. And you'll be lost. Proceed with caution.

Drink the Kool-Aid

To blindly accept something without taking in the full extent of its laxative effects. Examples of such behaviour are plumping for the cheapest caterers for your work social or accepting your eighth coffee of the day so as not to appear inferior to 'Mike the Caffeine King'.

E

Eat the elephant one bite at a time

Another way of saying 'let's break this down into small, manageable steps'. It's a great phrase to use when your assistant asks you for a pay rise for the fifth time. You could say:

> *Woah there, Shivani, you've only been here for six years, let's just eat this elephant one bite at a time, shall we?*

Elevator pitch

A two-minute speech that must have the perfect balance of information and entertainment. Before sharing your idea, take yourself out of your everyday life and pretend you're in a prime-time TV show. Imagine the camera close-up on your face capturing every bead of sweat and accidental bit of spittle, listen to the music slowly building to a crescendo as your overarching point starts to become clear. This is your moment to convince, persuade and, if necessary, hypnotise your colleagues, in order to get what you want.

The trick is to hide your true feelings about the idea behind a veil of drama, constant eye contact and possibly even outlandish props.

Empower

This is the best term to use if there's a task that needs doing, which you really don't want to do. Anybody who's anybody knows that the way to empower others is to subtly get them to do your job for you. As a leader of the future, your ability to empower will only improve over time. Be sure to hand over control, but hold on tight to the reins of approval. Your colleagues can implement their ideas, but it will be *you* who takes the credit for having the initiative to ask *them* in the first place. It's a win-win for everybody.

See also: *Win-win* and *Mentor*.

End of the day

A period of time that gets a lot of airtime, but nobody is quite sure *when* it is. It's a mythical period where people stop caring about everything and nothing matters.

At the end of the day, it doesn't affect anything.

At the end of the day, it's all irrelevant.

At the end of the day, it's all utter nonsense.

If only we could actually *get* there ...

Escalate

Quite often, threatening to escalate a situation has an even better effect than actually escalating it to your manager or manager's manager. In the workplace, the words 'I don't want to, but I'm going to have to escalate this ...' have as much power as 'I'm going to tell my mum/ dad/legal guardian' had in the playground. Use it sparingly, though.

Fire up the engine on this

This is a declaration of intent to ignite enthusiasm from your overwhelmed and undervalued team. It means:

> *Let's get started on this by making a lot of noise, drawing attention to ourselves, but doing so in a super-sexy firefighter way.*
> *Go team!*

To really ramp up the energy, start playing a siren recording on your phone while squirting water into the faces of your colleagues.

Follow from the middle

Following from the middle is the new 'leading from the front'. It means that you soak up the ideas of those around you and create a swarm. This way, your co-workers become your bodyguards without even realising it, and if an idea of yours goes down badly, you can simply blame the swarm and fly away.

Gaining traction

When you finally get a project moving after months of stagnation, this is a moment to celebrate. Whether you're in first gear, you're moving so fast you're knocking down unwitting pedestrians or you're reversing round and round a roundabout, be sure to let your boss

know that you feel like you're really gaining some traction.

Feel the wind in your hair.

Gamechanger

The game is always the same, no matter the players. But occasionally, something comes along that feels familiar, yet different enough that it can be labelled 'a gamechanger'. You can start claiming that 'the landscape has now completely altered' (even if it hasn't) and 'people are going to do things totally differently now' (even if they won't). The rumour that this change is so radical that the fabric of society will be woven anew can be started – by you, of course. Seize your moment.

See also: *Paradigm shift*.

Get down in the weeds

Sadly, there's no glory to be had from getting down in the weeds – going over and over the unattractive details that ultimately bog you down and keep you far away from the flowers that you really want to be tending. If you complain loudly enough about how far down in the weeds you are, hopefully they'll hear you and hire a gardener – or at least buy you a gnome.

Get into bed with

Much less fun than it sounds, to 'get into bed' with someone signifies becoming more familiar with them on a *strictly professional level*. But you should never use this phrase on the person you're hoping to become better acquainted with, as the nuance may be lost and you'll most likely find yourself in some sort of tribunal.

Get these wagons circling

When danger is on the horizon, you need to get your team into a defensive position. This could be taken figuratively, or literally – it doesn't matter. You could up the blood pressure and adrenalin flow of your team by getting them to move around on their wheelie chairs as quickly as possible in a circular motion. This will not only increase the level of hysteria in the air, but it will

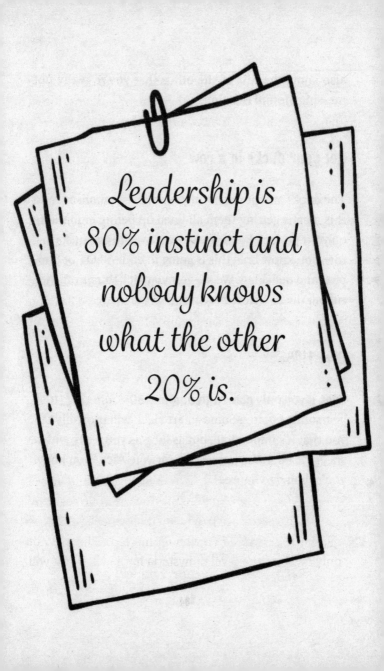

Leadership is 80% instinct and nobody knows what the other 20% is.

also show the rest of the office that you're really not messing around this time.

Get your ducks in a row

The ducks are the details of your plan (symbolism), and this means getting them all lined up before embarking on your project. But if you've ever tried to get ducks in a row, you know how this is going to end. A LOT of flapping and quacking. We suggest you kick things off with rubber ducks before moving on to the living.

Give 110%

Even if you only plan to give around 30%, offering 110% just sounds better. Some smart aleck will probably tell you that it's impossible, but as long as you reply with a sneer, 'It might be impossible for *you*, Alec,' you know you're going to impress.

Give them the sizzle but not the sausage!

This is the idea that people prefer the anticipation of hearing the sizzle of a sausage cooking to the actual sausage itself. The term was possibly created by someone with an underwhelming sausage. Or a vegan.

Remember this phrase when you're asked to give a round-up of a project, so you are reminded to focus on giving a very light overview of the positives without sharing anything of any substance. It's what they want.

Gravy train

This is a job that is easy but earns you tons of cash. When discussing 'riding the gravy train', a traditional 'yee haa' should help to get your point across. Colleagues will be forming an orderly queue to get on board with you as it sounds so warm and delicious.

Hard stop

There are stops – and there are hard stops. If your meeting has a 'hard stop' for 3pm and somebody tries to say something at 3.01pm, just put your palm over their face until they get the message. Or play some very loud 'exit music' on your phone.

Helicopter view

If you're caught hovering around the office making small talk with colleagues from various departments, just say you're trying to get the helicopter view of that latest project, even when what you're really doing is sampling all the biscuits.

Hit the ground running

If you say in a job interview that you'll hit the ground running, it'll sound to your employer like you actually go running, which will sound like you have a go-getting attitude and a lot of energy. Nobody will realise until it's too late that you'll actually spend the first few weeks falling flat on your face and asking for one of those foil emergency blankets.

Hitch-hike on the back of that comment

Asking somebody if you can 'hitch-hike on the back of' their comment is like asking them for a lift while wielding a weapon. There's no way they can say no. You're openly acknowledging that you're pretty much just repeating what they said, letting them do the work while you put your feet up, sing along to the radio and enjoy the ride. But you're saying it with style and while threatening violence, so no one will dare stop you.

Holistic overview

Being in touch with your spiritual side is something you should reference sporadically to make your colleagues think there's so much more to you than meets the eye. Saying you're interested in getting the 'holistic overview' of a project is a *spiritual* way of saying you want to analyse external factors that could affect the profitability level and outcome. To give your performance that extra pizazz, wear yoga pants, bring your own acupuncture needles to the next pow-wow and offer out free chanting sessions to your colleagues. You could say:

> *If we don't analyse every detail of ourselves, we'll never achieve anything. Now have some green tea.*

Homing from work

This is the art of dealing with personal life admin in the workplace. It can include things like arranging your best friend's hen/stag do or loudly booking a *very* private wax in an open-plan office.

I

Ideate

Making verbs from nouns is something Shakespeare used to do. And people think he's smart. Seeing as 'brainstorm' has lost its wow factor and 'thought shower' is lame and creepy, why not get your colleagues together and ideate? And don't forget to claim credit as the ideator for anything good that comes from the meeting.

I hear what you are saying ...

... but I wish I couldn't.

Remember to say the first part out loud, but the second part just to yourself.

Imagineer

Just like a lot of the phrases in this book, this is a word that doesn't need to exist. But it's bound to impress someone. If you invent anything at all – be it Bow-Tie Tuesdays, Wellington Wednesdays, or any other form of forced fashion fun – *you*, friend, are an Imagineer. Be sure to add it to your business cards so people start to think of you as some kind of magician.

Inflection point

In differential calculus and geometry, an inflection point is what's known as the point on a smooth plane curve at which the curvature changes sign. In the case of the graph of a function, it is a point where the function changes from being concave to convex, or vice versa.

In business, an inflection point is when SHIT STARTS HAPPENING. And by shit, we mean *anything*. Feel free to say, 'I feel like we're approaching the inflection point' as many times as you like throughout the lifetime of the project.

Inspiration Boulevard

The opposite of Green Day's boulevard of broken dreams, Inspiration Boulevard is where dreams are made. Whether it's a real boulevard, a back alley or the place you go when you close your eyes, talk about it with the same reverence people usually reserve to discuss their gap year. 'This one time, I took a stroll down my Inspiration Boulevard and, I mean you probably had to be there, but ...'

Issues

I got 99 issues but not a single problem. Because in the corporate world a 'problem' will send everyone into a tailspin, so we don't have them. Ever. (NB. Yes, a 'normal' dictionary will tell you they mean the same thing, but a corporate dictionary would never make such a foolish mistake.)

The broader your stance, the higher your pay packet.

It's on my radar

Is a polite way of saying 'Get off my back, Steve, you only asked me for that document eight weeks ago, give me a BREAK, man!' The trouble with keeping things on your radar for too long is that their beeping sound is so easily drowned out by those Britney tunes you insist on blasting out every day.

Joining the dots

If you're ever caught doodling on your notepad, just say 'I'm just joining the dots on our method going forward. I'm a really visual person.' Even when you've spent the last half hour drawing rabbits.

Journey

Ever heard the phrase: 'it's not about the destination, it's about the journey'? The business world has taken that and run wild with it. Everything is a journey – whether it's the process of your project from inception to completion, the decision of a consumer to buy your product or you going to do the tea run for your team – everything is a journey, and those journeys very rarely have a destination.

Juice isn't worth the squeeze

This means that something is simply too much effort to create a worthwhile outcome. It's essentially a more office-appropriate way of saying that you can't be bothered to use up your resources to complete an assignment that won't give you the recognition you require for that promotion.

Jump the shark

Jumping the shark is an attempt to salvage a company's reputation in a way that oozes desperation.

See also: *Re-brand* and *Balls in a jam jar*.

Keep your powder dry

Don't give away too much information. In the seventeenth century, this referred to the gunpowder soldiers had to keep dry in order to fight in battle. In the 1980s and 1990s, it referred to the drugs that businesspeople needed in order to seal *any* deal. In the twenty-first century, it refers to the makeup and protein powder that we all require in order to present a sweat-free, ripped version of ourselves.

Keynote speaker

Beware of anyone who says this is their main job title.

L

Let's fry some ideas in the thought wok and see what sizzles

In many ways, getting ahead in business is like cooking a meal – winging it and hoping for the best is often the only way to get food on your table. Essentially, this is another way of saying:

> *Chuck it all in and see what happens because I have no idea what I'm doing.*

But in the guise of a carefree and creative attitude ...

What did I do at
the weekend?
It's none of
your business,
Jeremy.

Light-touch meeting

You might ask: 'What's the point of meeting if we can't touch each other?' And for that, you would be reprimanded. These days, a 'light-touch meeting' simply means a more relaxed, informal atmosphere. But do not be fooled into thinking this is actually any different to a normal meeting. You can smile more, but you still need to be on your guard.

Look under the bonnet

Have a peek at the inner workings of something, pretend to understand them, before quietly replacing the lid and calling a mechanic.

Low-hanging fruit

In the business world, picking low-hanging fruit means doing the easiest work first for a quick win. If you're having a weekly catch-up with your team, rattle off all the simple tasks you have achieved so there's little time left to get into the nitty gritty of those larger projects you should have begun months ago. When the situation gets really desperate, bring in a fruit basket to distract them.

HOW TO OUT-RIDDLE A RIDDLER AND OTHER USEFUL TIPS

Not only does the working world have its own language, it also has its own unique and often contradictory rules. It takes years, sometimes decades, to fully understand them, but this section should give you a head start and save you at least a few weeks of ruminating.

Out-riddling a riddler

If you've asked Ben a question, and you get the sense he's trying to riddle you, just reply with any of the following:

- [ ] Yell 'WHAT'S YOUR POINT, BEN?' across the room.
- [ ] Quietly, but continuously, shush him.
- [ ] Slam your fist on the table and mutter to yourself, 'Well, that does it.'

Well, that does it ...

Speaking metaphorically

If you want to get out of answering a difficult question, start speaking in metaphors and analogies using the first topic that comes into your head, no matter the relevance to the original question. For example:

'You know, sometimes, you just have to let the nightingales migrate to see if you even want them to return.'

'What we should really be asking ourselves is, why do seagulls have so much more to say than we do?'

'It's just like when a kingfisher arrives to take its place by the stream, all the other wildlife notices, doesn't it?'

Being a new joiner

Part of becoming a successful leader is learning to master the art of small talk. Here are a few ice-breakers to try out the next time you're joining a new team. Do your best to squeeze all of these questions into the first ten minutes after your arrival – people will marvel at your ability to fill every silence, so don't worry if you feel like the conversation doesn't have a clear direction:

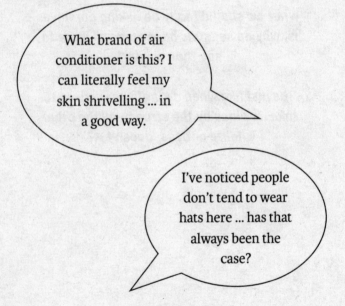

What brand of air conditioner is this? I can literally feel my skin shrivelling ... in a good way.

I've noticed people don't tend to wear hats here ... has that always been the case?

What's your perfect Tuesday?

How many daily vitamin D supplements do you need to survive here?

What's that? No, not that, that. Over there.

Where did your watercoolers used to be?

What GSM is that piece of paper? It looks strong ...

Which is your favourite acronym?

Before you start with the team, it's a great idea to 'connect' with them all on LinkedIn and endorse every skill they have listed on their profiles even before you've met them. It'll show everybody what a supportive team player you are.

Knowing all of the words

If somebody says a phrase that you don't understand, do not, under any circumstances, admit to not knowing what it means. Instead, adopt it into your everyday lexicon and say it with a smirk.

Compliments to pay your colleagues before asking for their help

Once you've got to know the team, it's important to keep them onside so you can start palming your work off onto them tout suite ... If none of the below openers are quite right for your request, don't forget that a warm, lingering smile can also go a long way.

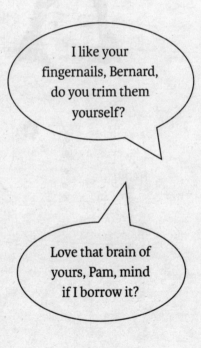

Celia, I don't care what everybody else says, I'd never put you down as a Hufflepuff. Now, about those charts ...

Everybody says you're really creative ... can I get your help with something?*

* FACT: *Everybody* believes they are an undervalued creative genius. By telling somebody they are creative before asking for their help, you are challenging them to prove they can live up to their own impossibly high expectations.

Bathroom banter

This might come as a surprise to you, but at some point in your career you will have to use the office bathroom. Annoyingly, your colleagues will occasionally need to do the same thing, at exactly the same time. Social skills are truly tested in these situations so it's best to have a few openers up your sleeve to fill those dreaded 30 seconds of pre-, post- or mid-pee and -poop.

If, for whatever reason, you find yourself stumped, remember that a double-handed wave to show that you're friendly *and* you've washed your hands is always a great back-up.

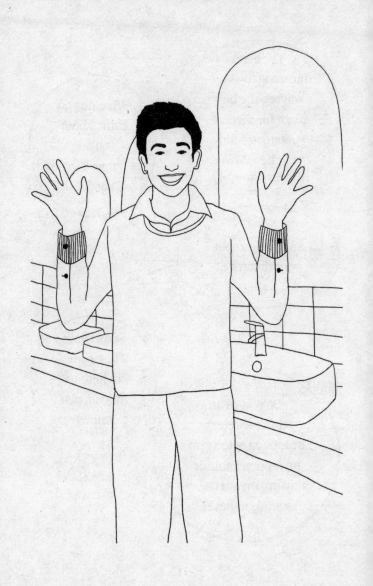

Magic bullet

This is a miracle solution that will GET YOU WHERE YOU WANT TO GO faster and harder than other solutions.

Magic hour

The very last hour of the working day when you finally make a start on your to-do list.
    See also: *Close of play*.

Make hay

First recorded in John Heywood's *A Dialogue conteinyng the number in effect of all the Prouerbes in the Englishe Tongue*, 1546.

> *Whan the sunne shinth make hay.*
> *Whiche is to say.*
> *Take time whan time cometh,*
> *lest time steale away.*

We're pretty sure John Heywood was talking about using your business downtime to update your CV and LinkedIn to plan your next move.

Marzipan layer

This is the layer of management just below the top. They're as slippery and slimy as they sound. They are not to be trusted.

Mentee

Somebody who is seemingly thirsty to learn from a person who is more experienced, but who, 90% of the time, is there to point out how archaic and outdated everybody else's methods are. The trick to being a good mentee is to keep the eye-rolling to a minimum and appear outwardly engaged and impressed.

Mentor

Somebody who is seemingly selfless, willing to give up their time to progress your career, but in fact is there to steal your very best ideas and present them as their own. A good mentor will apologise immediately after pitching your idea to the wider team, but first they will make sure nobody is around to overhear them.

Mission critical

If you need to motivate a member of your team, tell them that their input is 'mission critical'. It makes your project sound incredibly important – like you're going to space to save the burning planet rather than just sell-ing a product the world will forget in five years' time. If the situation is really desperate, fork out on a NASA T-shirt.

Moving the goalposts

Changing the aim, blurring the focus, bewildering the team. It's what leaders do best.

Nail jelly to the wall

Used to describe something that is impossible, pointless and, above all, is really going to annoy the cleaners.

See also: *Boil an ocean*.

Narrative

Instead of asking, 'what's our story?', ask 'what's our narrative?', so that it sounds a bit more cinematic and artsy and gets people in the mood for popcorn.

A company's 'narrative' is the tale its workers make up by way of attaching a 'success story' to their otherwise soulless brand. Every company tells a story because all working adults were once children, and children are notorious fans of stories – particularly those involving incremental economic gain every quarter. Remember to include a bit of peril at the midpoint to really ramp up the drama, so that your audience feels genuinely relieved when you finally reach the resolution.

And then, right when we thought we'd lost it all, we not only made our budget but opened seven new offices in Brazil.
The End.

Negative growth

If you find that you've accidentally cost your company thousands, or even millions, of pounds, you can talk about the loss in terms of 'negative growth' so that it sounds as though *something* – even if it's just the knowledge that somebody else should be put in charge next time – has been gained from the whole experience.

Let's not focus on what we haven't earned,
but instead on what we've learned.

Next slide please

Use this to show that you're not only in control of the presentation, but also the amount of time your colleagues have to spend sitting through it. You want to go back a slide? You can. You want to stay on the same slide for 16 minutes? You can do that, too.

If you're actually operating the slides yourself, use this term anyway to make it seem like you have an assistant hiding somewhere in the room poised to respond to your commands.

Not enough bandwidth

It's fine to admit/claim that you've got too much to do, but if you say 'not enough bandwidth, sorry' instead of your usual 'the food keeps falling off all these plates I'm spinning', you'll seem much more technologically savvy and much less like an incompetent circus act.

Observations

As in, 'Your pitch was great, I just have a few observations ...' To the untrained ear, this sounds fairly innocuous, but it heralds an onslaught of criticism about everything from the font you're using or the way you styled your hair to everything you stand for. When you hear it, brace yourself. But when you're in the judge's

seat it's a useful tool for your arsenal, enabling you to get away with complete character annihilation while keeping things friendly.

Offlining

If you suggest 'offlining' something, it sounds like you're just wanting to take the topic offline, but in reality you're striking it down there and then in the hope that it won't ever be resurrected.

Out of the loop

This isn't somewhere you ever want to be, unless it involves planning the next staff social, of course. If that's the case, get yourself out of there faster than you can say 'loop the loop'.

P

Paradigm shift

If you've already used 'gamechanger' to describe your latest four or five ideas that have since turned out to be duds, it's time to switch things up before people start openly accusing you of lying. A paradigm shift sounds new *and* a little frightening, so you're bound to get the thrill-seekers on board, no matter how terrible your suggestion is.

Like a lot of the phrases in this book, its impact relies heavily on your ability to say it with a straight face.

Peel the onion

If you want to peel the onion of a project, you want to delve into it, one layer at a time, so you can figure out which layers are the most stressful and therefore most likely to make you cry. These are the parts you're going to want to hand over to your nearest colleague. You might say:

I was peeling the onion on the latest spring project over the weekend and I thought your strengths, Mo, would really lend themselves to the core ... No, don't cry, it's going to be fine ...

Pile on

A pile on is when somebody suggests something in a meeting and the rest of the team collectively decide to unleash all the frustration from their personal lives onto that person. No matter how great their suggestion ... If you're the person at the receiving end of the pile on, don't even try to fight them, just nod and smile as each individual vents at you, then bring the idea back at the next meeting, when it'll be sure to sail through.

Ping-pong with the big hitters

Way, way, way back in the late twentieth century, business deals were fuelled by a constant supply of booze and banter, and businessfolk rarely set foot into offices. Golf courses, fancy restaurants, squash courts – you name it, businessfolk frequented them during work time. Today, however, no other business location is held in higher esteem than the ping-pong court. If you want to make real money, invest in a sweat band and start working on your backhand topspin ASAP.

Pivot

More subtle than a U-turn, less destructive than a full reversal, saying 'We've decided to pivot in a different direction' translates as 'We can see now that our first idea belongs in the bin.' But it makes it sound strategic.

Play hardball

Don't even think about suggesting playing softball. If your team gets a whiff of your desire for fair, gentle play to prevent anybody getting bruised, you'll never make it through the working week.

Now say it with us: 'I am strong. I am tough. I am threatening. I want to play hardball.'

Punch the puppy

To do something morally bad in order to benefit the business. If the business world was in the habit of telling it how it is, every company's logo would feature a sad puppy and their motto would read: *Lie, cheat, steal ... but don't get caught.*

Put on a record to see who dances

To try something simply to see what happens. Working days can be long and repetitive, so pumping out your favourite tunes every now and then is a great way to inject some energy into the office floor. If any clients

Lie, cheat, steal...
but don't get caught

stop by while your team is 'experimenting', encourage them to join in too.

Come on, Jaz, the instrumental section is coming. It's time to freestyle!

Q1, Q2, Q3, Q4

Never, under any circumstances, refer to the seasons of the year by name, because nobody will know what the hell you're talking about. Remember when Bryan Adams was singing about the summer of '69 and Johnny Rivers was banging on about summer rain?* Nor us, but apparently they were just talking about a particularly tumultuous Q3.

* 'Why are these song references from the sixties?' you might ask. Well, to be a leader in the eyes of your older colleagues, it's vital that you understand their references and strange jokes. Be sure to brush up on some ancient cultural history so you can join in.

Quick win

A quick win is an action that secures a visible contribution to the success of a business. New employees often want to bag a quick win as soon as possible to reassure their employers that they made the right decision in hiring them. However, sometimes what appears to be a quick win on the surface can very quickly turn into a quick lose.

To be on the safe side, we suggest you use your probation period to tell people that you're 'really gaining traction' on something and then go in for the win as soon as it's more difficult for them to fire you. Just in case.

See also: *Gaining traction.*

Quiet shuffle away

A quiet shuffle away in the business world is what 'ghosting' is to the dating world. Instead of dealing with a problem head on like a mature, well-respected adult, you can either carpet-shuffle out of a meeting or, even more spinelessly, simply stop replying to emails from a particular contact. Then at the next networking event where you inevitably see said contact, pretend that what you had between you fell apart due to unforeseen circumstances that were totally out of your control. Or just avoid them and down the free wine.

R

Reach out

Instead of getting in contact with someone, why not try 'reaching out'? It implies so much more effort on your part. You could say:

> *I reached out to Jay all the way in*
> *Kazakhstan, and he said he might be*
> *interested ...*

Real-time

If you want to talk about things in real time you need to say so. If you're saying 'a month' and you actually mean a month, make sure you clarify so people don't confuse it with that other kind of time we sometimes operate in.

Re-brand

A re-brand is a way of reinventing something in order to get a little attention. It's a bit like when a toddler starts dressing up and behaving differently when a new, unwanted, sibling arrives on the scene. To placate the re-branders, keep reassuring them that this is a really exciting time while ignoring the sense of desperation they are trying so hard to conceal.

Retrograding

This is post-project analysis in a painfully slow way masquerading as a fun and exciting one. It's an opportunity to look back at the mistakes that everybody made in the last project and awkwardly apportion blame, even when deep down you all know it was Tim's fault.

Let's do a bit of retrograding here.
Tim, you in?

Rolling the tortoise

Everybody knows that if you want to hurry a tortoise along, you need as many people as possible to gently encourage it. Just like in the business world, when you have a slow-moving project, the best way to progress it is to involve ten more people. 'Won't that just create more opinions, longer meetings and further delays?' we hear you ask. Yes, yes it might. You could say:

> *I know we recruited five people last week to work on the H.A.R.E. project but I think we're going to need another fifty to really get this tortoise rolling.*

Ronseal

Quite simply, does what it says on the tin.

> *That's Ronseal, baby!*

Run it up the flagpole

Throw an idea out there to see what your colleagues think of it. You could buy a flagpole and dance around it like it's May Day until somebody notices and asks you to stop, but only do that if you're *really* committed.

Shit sandwich

- Compliment
- Criticism
- Compliment

Of course, even if the bread you're using is your local bakery's finest rustic sourdough, you know all they're going to do is taste the shit. But at least you can feel satisfied that you tried to soften the blow.

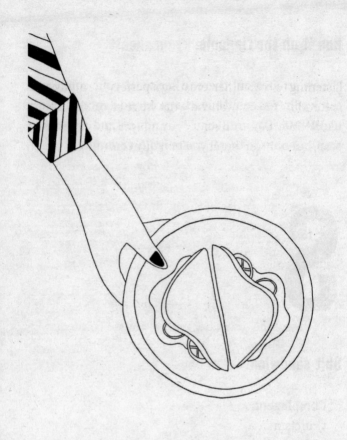

Singing from the same hymn sheet

Listening to each other, creating a perfect harmony and pretending to comprehend what we're all talking about are all key to becoming a team player. Shout-singing over your colleagues and taking it to the bridge when everybody just wants to do the chorus again are habits that you're going to have to kick if you want to make it to the semi-finals of this talent show.

Soup to nuts

A whole project viewed as a meal – from the starter, right the way through to the final course before we all hit up the bathroom.

Square the circle

See: *Boil an ocean* and *Nail jelly to the wall*.

Strategic staircase

This is essentially a business plan that is supposed to be straightforward and with a very clear goal at the top. If your project starts to go awry and the next steps become less clear, the staircase morphs into a spiral to represent the dizzying, desperate and downright dangerous nature of your leadership. Hold on tight.

Sunset

Outside of the office, sunsets are beautiful, romantic, magical things to be admired. Inside, however, they have a much more sinister, murderous meaning ... You could pop on some sunglasses, grab a cigarette and say:

> *Mel, get the shotgun. We're going to sunset this project.*

Swim lanes

Your work swim lane is your everyday remit. It's important to make sure you stick to your lane or you might
suddenly feel a little passive-aggressive tap on your foot
for being too slow. If your lane feels too fast, remember
to ask for help or take 30 minutes in the jacuzzi to
reassess.

See also: *Bucketisation.*

Synergising

Bringing people or companies together to create a whole
that is greater than the sum of its parts is what synergis-
ing is all about. To ensure others understand your
meaning, it helps to clasp your hands together in front
of you David Brent-style when describing it.

T

Takeaways

Not to be confused with lovely, delicious meals, 'takeaways' are any key learnings we can summarise from a project. At the end of your next presentation try saying, *Hey, who wants a takeaway?* Watch your colleagues' eyes light up, then just start giving a summary of all your points while their expressions return to the usual vacant misery you're used to seeing, but now with an extra sprinkling of resentment.

Take it to the next level

If you're in a brainstorming meeting and can't think of anything useful to contribute, just say, *We really need something that's going to take this to the next level ...*

while looking out into the distance like some kind of business guru.

Your colleagues won't be able to stand the silence that follows and will fill it with any old mediocre suggestions, but with one eye on the guru in the room to see if you approve. Give the subtlest of nods at the strongest idea to really show who's in charge.

Think the unthinkable

Challenging your team to think of something that can't be thought of is a great motivator. Their desperation to appear as though they're on your unnavigable wavelength will force them to say anything at all.

Thirty-thousand-foot view

Looking at a situation as a whole instead of getting lost in all those teeny tiny 'important' details like profits and losses, budgets and debts, fines and fraud and prison.

See also: *Helicopter view*.

Tip of the spear

Ever heard the saying '*The tip of the spear strikes first*'? No? Really? Where have you been?! If you are described as the tip of the spear, it means you're a trailblazer. You're first in line to try a new venture. Actually, you're in line before a line has even formed behind you, so you're not even in line. You're so ahead of the game, you've completed the game before it's even been created, you know? You're in front of the curve at the end of the rainbow with the pot of gold, you know? You're ... what do you mean 'stop'?

Touch base offline

To discuss something at a later point. If you really want to throw your colleagues, use this while in a face-to-face meeting so they suddenly think they're being secretly live-streamed.

See also: *Circle back*.

Triangulate

To involve a third person in the discussion. You could say:

> *That sounds great but I'll just triangulate with Meera before confirming.*

You can upgrade this to include all of the shapes – 'rectangulate', 'pentagulate', 'hexagulate', 'septagulate', 'octagulate', 'nontagulate' are all totally acceptable words. Plus, it's fun to see your colleague trying to work out how many people you plan to involve.

Turnkey solutions

Ready to use, you just have to turn the key. Give your best estate agent's grin when delivering this one.

Understanding

If you skim-read a contract and glean that it's a good deal before you sign it, but later it turns out to be a terrible deal, instead of admitting you were very wrong, you can just say:

> *'My understanding was that it was a good deal.'* Nobody, but nobody, can argue with that.

Unknowns

Things we know that we don't know about yet.

SELF-DEPRECATION KILLS CAREERS. JUST STOP IT, JULIA.

Unknown unknowns

Things we don't know that we don't know about yet.

Unpack

To get to grips with something. To take it out of the suit-case and stare at it long and hard while wondering 'Why the hell did I buy that? Was it on offer ...?' You could say:

> *Let's unpack that and pop it on a hanger.*
> *Actually, do you know what? I'm just*
> *going to go ahead and put this on. Does*
> *anybody mind? I know it's a bit skimpy*
> *for the office ...*

Upskill

Instead of telling your assistant that they are in dire need of some training, encourage them to 'upskill' to make it seem that they already possess some skills even when it's very clear they have absolutely none at all.

Utilise

Why say 'use' when you can say 'utilise'?

Vertical

A vertical is a small market with a very specific audience that is being catered for by a niche idea. A good example of this is the readership of this book.

Visioning

Making a plan, describing something, literally thinking of anything new, can be described as 'visioning'.

See also: *Ideate*.

W

Weigh the pig

This describes spending ages analysing the performance of something instead of taking steps to grow the business.

See also: *Analysis paralysis*.

Where the rubber meets the road

The time or place at which something matters the most. Hold your breath and pray that no animals get harmed in the process.

Wiggle room

Building some wiggle room into any schedule will show your colleagues just how much you appreciate their need for time and space to wiggle.

Win-win

The holy grail of business, this is a situation in which both parties benefit. Of course, in reality there is only ever one winner in any business transaction, and you had better make sure it's you.

Workshop

To workshop something is to discuss and develop it in a safe environment. Just like in your school Design Technology classes, you can take your colleague's new initiative and gently chip away at it, sand it down, pull it apart, haphazardly stick it back together, throw on some varnish in the name of 'corporate strategy' until you're left with something ultimately not fit for purpose.

X

Theory X

This is the theory that suggests people hate working and are motivated by threats. NOW GET TO WORK OR YOU'RE GOING TO WISH YOU'D NEVER OPENED THIS BOOK!

See?

Y

Yardstick

An expression to describe something used for comparative purposes. Such as:

> *This spreadsheet is the yardstick of your overall performance.*

It's a good one to use in front of younger colleagues who have absolutely no idea what a yard is.

Gen-Y, -Z, -A

We don't know who we're marketing to, so let's just say 'everyone under the age of 40'. OK?

Z

Zero cycles

Another good term to use instead of saying that you're too busy. *I have zero cycles at the moment*, means I don't have time or resources to help you. Now back off.

See also: *Not enough bandwidth*.

Zero-tasking

If you're busy 'zero-tasking' you're doing zero tasks simultaneously. If you spend three hours staring at your to-do list with mild discomfort, congratulations, you are officially a zero-tasker!

Zombie project

A project that refuses to die, no matter how many times
people try to kill it.

BONUS BS BINGO
AND OTHER ACTIVITIES

Sometimes you find yourself in a meeting where you have literally *nothing* to say or do. Instead of awkwardly rearranging the position of your hands every five minutes to make them look less 'claw-like', have a go at a round of BS Bingo to pass the time until you can make your escape.

Simply tick off each phrase as you hear it. Make sure to do a low-key victory dance when you get a full house.

BS BINGO

CIRCLE BACK	GAMECHANGER
JOINING THE DOTS	ANALYSIS PARALYSIS
GAINING TRACTION	LOW-HANGING FRUIT
MISSION CRITICAL	PLAY HARDBALL

ESCALATE	BUCKETISATION
DEEP DIVE	TAKE IT TO THE NEXT LEVEL
SQUARE THE CIRCLE	UNKNOWN UNKNOWNS
BOIL AN OCEAN	NEXT SLIDE PLEASE

BS WORDSEARCH

Wordsearches might seem like a waste of time, but so is about 80% of your working day, so just do this and try to enjoy it:

☐ BACKBURNER

☐ HARD STOP

☐ IDEATE

☐ MAGIC BULLET

☐ PUNCH THE PUPPY

☐ RONSEAL

☐ WIN WIN

☐ ZOMBIE PROJECT

J	N	X	D	I	T	C	E	O	Z	P	N
R	O	Z	B	L	M	H	S	A	O	U	Y
S	B	E	O	V	A	R	D	Y	M	M	P
L	E	A	F	O	G	Q	W	A	B	S	P
A	T	T	C	W	I	E	V	L	I	G	U
E	A	G	E	K	C	S	B	Z	E	B	P
S	E	L	A	T	B	X	H	K	P	Q	E
N	D	L	S	E	U	U	A	P	R	B	H
O	I	R	G	I	L	B	R	D	O	C	T
R	F	W	R	C	L	K	D	N	J	P	H
M	Q	B	N	P	E	F	S	H	E	S	C
B	U	O	R	I	T	O	T	W	C	R	N
T	R	X	M	A	W	G	O	X	T	V	U
S	P	W	O	F	V	J	P	I	U	E	P

BS WIND DOWN

Five minutes to go before you can make an exit for lunch? Use that time wisely by colouring in these printers and photocopiers using only the colour grey.

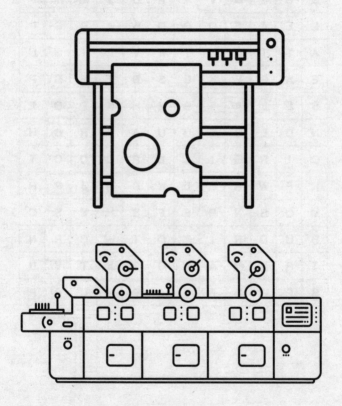

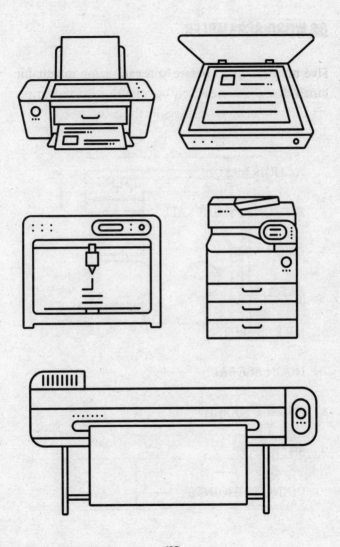

BS WORD SCRAMBLER

Unscramble these words to reveal some invaluable phrases:

1. WITCH AND HISS

2. A CHOIR MUG

3. ZIT ZONES SLEAT KALL

4. REIGN AIME

5. EAT SCALE

6. MR RAIN BOTS

7. NOON ACE BAIL

8. ENGAGE MARCH

9. SHARD POT

10. DOING THE JOINTS

Answers:

1. SHIT SANDWICH; 2. MAGIC HOUR; 3. ALL SIZZLE
NO STEAK; 4. IMAGINEER; 5. ESCALATE;
6. BRAINSTORM; 7. BOIL AN OCEAN;
8. GAMECHANGER; 9. HARD STOP; 10. JOINING
THE DOTS

IMPLEMENTING BS IN EVERY SITUATION

Join the correct phrase to the situation.

You've been asked a question you don't know the answer to.

You need a colleague to do something for you.

You want to inject some enthusiasm into your exhausted team.

You want to repeat a colleague's good point.

You've been asked to do something you don't want to do.

You want to try something but have absolutely no idea if it will work.

I really want you to feel empowered today, so ...

Let's fire up the engine on this!

Not enough bandwidth, sorry!

We're in serious danger of analysis paralysis, people.

It's time to put on a record to see who dances.

Great, I'm just going to hitch-hike on the back of that comment.

BS PRESENTATION TOOL

Fill or simply colour in the gaps of this unnecessarily complicated flowchart to work out how you plan to ideate the next paradigm shift, in order to really start gaining some traction on that new project you were supposed to begin a month ago. Be sure to include the completed flowchart in your next mediocre presentation.

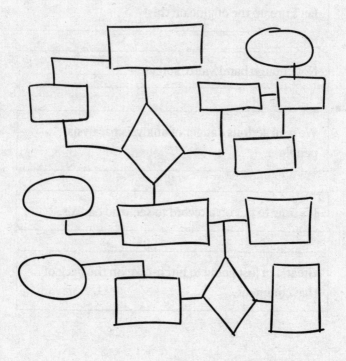

ADD YOUR OWN BS PHRASES

If you discover a new, particularly effective phrase which hasn't featured in this dictionary, please do add it in the space below.

....

_____

_____

_____

....

_____

_____

_____